THE SIDE

Ghosts
and Other Spectres

A book of monstrous beings from the dark side of myths
and legends around the world, illustrated by David West and
written by Anita Ganeri

WAYLAND

This edition published in 2012 by Wayland

Wayland
Hachette Children's Books
338 Euston Road
London NW1 3BH

Wayland Australia
Level 17/207 Kent Street
Sydney, NSW 2000

Produced by

David West ☂☂ Children's Books
7 Princeton Court
55 Felsham Road
London SW15 1AZ

Designer: Gary Jeffrey
Editor: Katharine Pethick
Illustrator: David West

A CIP catalogue record for this book is available from the British Library.

ISBN: 9780750267786

Printed in China

Wayland is a division of Hachette Children's Books, an Hachette UK company
www.hachette.co.uk

Picture credits:
8b, Angelhead; 12b, 14l, Library of Congress; 15b, Pilgab; 20b, LuckyLouie; 21-22, Paul Keleher; 21b, Tomascastelazo

Contents

Introduction

Many bizarre creatures roam the world of mythology. Their origins may be lost in the mists of history, but they have preyed on people's superstitions and imaginations since ancient times. Among them are ghosts and spectres, supernatural beings from the dark side that appear in the living world. Although they cannot be touched or felt, their presence is terrifying. For thousands of years, people claim to have seen ghosts but what are these mysterious figures? Many believe that they are the souls of the dead, come back to haunt the land of the living. Have you ever seen a ghost? Or a poltergeist? Are you ready to go over to the dark side? It will send shivers down your spine...

Ghosts

In the spooky, gloomy twilight of a graveyard, a hideous figure emerges from the earth. It is a ghost, returning to the world of the living – the world in which you live.

The idea of ghosts is thousands of years old. This is a scene from the Old Testament of the Bible – the ghost of the prophet Samuel is summoned by the Witch of Endor.

People from cultures all over the world believe that a person's soul survives when his or her body dies. But sometimes the soul stays in the land of the living, perhaps because the person died in some terrible way, or wants to take revenge on somebody who is still alive. In western cultures, this soul is said to haunt a place or a person – and is seen as ghost.

A typical medieval image of the ghost – in medieval times, when death was commonplace, people were terrified by the prospect of the dead returning to them.

Ghostly Features

What do you think a ghost looks like? Is it a white, transparent human figure clad in robes? Some ghosts are said to look like this, but some are invisible and some are not even human.

Eyewitnesses often say that ghosts appear to be made of cloudy, fog-like material, so that they are see-through. That is how ghosts normally appear in photographs. Ghosts cannot be touched – you could put your hand right through a ghost. They can walk through solid objects – walls and doors included – so hiding in a room is no defence. Ghosts normally take the form of the dead person as they were last seen, so someone who died by being beheaded may appear without a head or may even be seen carrying their head under their arm!

Any ghostly image is known as an apparition. It may be visible to one person but not another. This photograph, taken by the medium William Hope (1863-1933), is said to show a man with the ghost of his wife.

This bizarre image shows a substance apparently coming from the ear of a medium who is in contact with the spirit world. The substance is known as ectoplasm and is said to make up the ghostly body of a spirit.

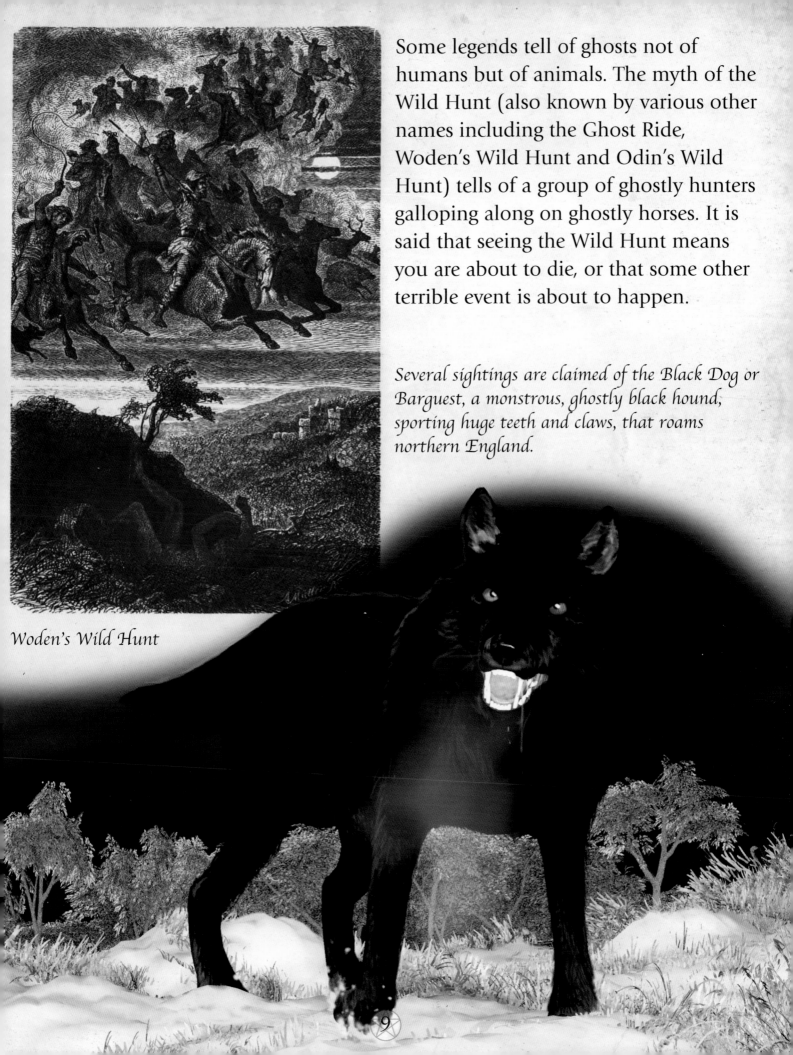

Some legends tell of ghosts not of humans but of animals. The myth of the Wild Hunt (also known by various other names including the Ghost Ride, Woden's Wild Hunt and Odin's Wild Hunt) tells of a group of ghostly hunters galloping along on ghostly horses. It is said that seeing the Wild Hunt means you are about to die, or that some other terrible event is about to happen.

Several sightings are claimed of the Black Dog or Barguest, a monstrous, ghostly black hound, sporting huge teeth and claws, that roams northern England.

Woden's Wild Hunt

Ghosts in Europe

Ghosts have appeared in the folklore of European countries since ancient times, when the Greeks and Romans thought that ghosts hung around burial places, doing both good and evil deeds.

An apparition in an English country garden

The Greeks invited the ghosts of their relatives and friends to lavish feasts. A shade was a type of ghost that featured in classical Greek stories, including Homer's Odyssey. Shades are spirits of the Greek underworld, which live in the shadows after death. In Roman mythology, manes (meaning 'the good ones') were the souls of the dead. They were offered blood sacrifices, sometimes at gladiatorial games. The annual festival for manes was held on February 19th.

A typical woman ghost, often called the White Lady (or sometimes the Grey Lady). She always appears in a long white dress.

In the Middle Ages, Europeans believed that souls went to purgatory until, as ghosts, they could make amends for their sins in life.

A White Lady formed from ectoplasm (see page 8).

In Britain, the White Lady is the name for a female ghost. The White Lady is often the ghost of a woman who has killed herself after losing her husband. If the White Lady appears in a family home, it means another member of the family is about to die. The Knights of Alleberg are the ghosts of twelve Swedish knights who died at the battle at Alleberg in 1389. They are said to be resting until their country needs them to fight again.

Ghosts Around theWorld

Ghostly figures are found in legends from all over the world, both ancient and modern. In addition, ghosts are often a feature of places of death, such as places of execution, battlefields and shipwrecks.

The battlefields of the American Civil War are said to be haunted by the ghosts of the fallen. At Gettysburg, where nearly 8,000 soldiers died in 1863, dozens of visitors have reported seeing ghostly wounded men and hearing the grisly sounds of battle. From native North American culture comes the chindi, a ghost of the Navajo people. It is said to leave a dying person's body with their last breath.

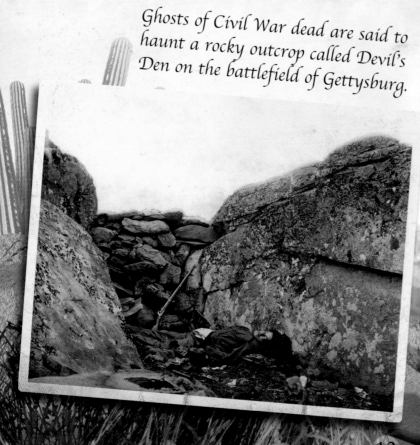

Ghosts of Civil War dead are said to haunt a rocky outcrop called Devil's Den on the battlefield of Gettysburg.

Navajo legend says that if a person meets a chindi, he or she falls ill with 'ghost sickness'.

In Japan, a funayurei is the ghost of a person who died at sea.

The Obambo is a ghost of Central Africa. When the Obambo asks its relatives to build it a home, villagers hold a ceremony, visit the grave of the dead person and build a small hut for the Obambo. In Japan, a yurei is the ghost of a person who dies a violent death. It appears in white funeral robes and has black hair and lifeless hands and feet.

China has many different types of ghost. Hungry ghosts are created when people who are greedy in life die. They gradually become weak and disappear.

Haunted Houses

Ghostly figures roam many haunted houses, castles, theatres and other buildings around the world. These ghosts are the souls of people who have died terrible deaths in the buildings.

The house in Amityville, USA, that was the scene of a terrifying haunting in the 1970s. The family who lived here fled. The haunting was the subject of a famous book and film, The Amityville Horror.

In 1974, at 112 Ocean Avenue in the American town of Amityville, Ronald DeFeo murdered his family as they slept. A year later the Lutz family moved into the house. But four weeks later, they moved out again, claiming that the house was haunted – perhaps by DeFeo's victims. Windows had opened and closed by themselves, doors had been ripped off their hinges and slime had oozed through the ceilings. Mr Lutz had even been levitated above his bed.

The ghost of ex-president Abraham Lincoln (left) is supposed to wander the corridors of the White House (below), knocking on doors. He is also seen in the room where his old bed is kept.

Borden House in Massachusetts, USA, is said to be haunted by the ghosts of two people murdered there in 1892.

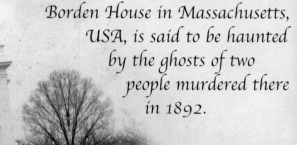

Borley Rectory in Essex is known as the most haunted house in England. Reverend Smith's family lived there in the 1920s. They heard bells and footsteps, and saw lights and a ghostly horse-drawn carriage on the drive. Numerous ghosts are said to haunt the Tower of London. They include King Edward V and his brother the Duke of York, who were murdered here as children. Other Tower ghosts include Anne Boleyn, second wife of Henry VIII, who was beheaded in 1536.

The ghost of a nun was often seen walking in the grounds of Borley Rectory, England. She was seen by four girls living there in 1900. The rectory burned down in 1939.

The ghosts of two royal princes, murdered in 1483, have been seen, walking hand in hand, in the Tower of London.

The two princes

The Brown Lady haunts the staircase of Raynham Hall in Norfolk. She is the ghost of Lady Townshend.

Ghost Ships

Humans and animals are not the only ghosts. Ghostly ships sail the oceans and ghostly trains run through the countryside. Most famous is a strange ship sailed by its ghostly captain – the Flying Dutchman.

The legend of the Flying Dutchman tells of a ship that was sunk during a storm near the Cape of Good Hope in 1641. The Flying Dutchman was its skipper, Captain Vanderdecken. As the ship went down, Vanderdecken cried out that he would pass the Cape, even if he had to sail until the end of time. And so he sails around the Cape to this day. A sighting of the Flying Dutchman on his vessel is supposed to be a sign of impending disaster.

During the Second World War, the crew of a German submarine reported seeing a ghostly ship passing close by – was it the famous Flying Dutchman?

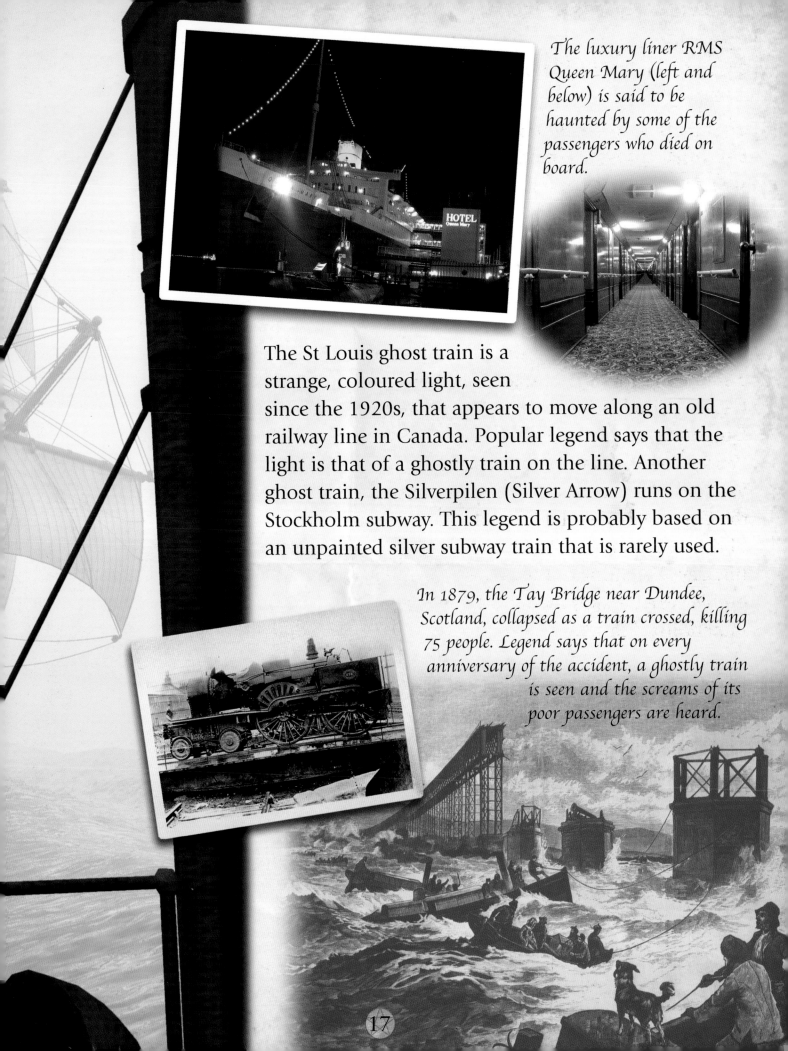

The luxury liner RMS Queen Mary (left and below) is said to be haunted by some of the passengers who died on board.

The St Louis ghost train is a strange, coloured light, seen since the 1920s, that appears to move along an old railway line in Canada. Popular legend says that the light is that of a ghostly train on the line. Another ghost train, the Silverpilen (Silver Arrow) runs on the Stockholm subway. This legend is probably based on an unpainted silver subway train that is rarely used.

In 1879, the Tay Bridge near Dundee, Scotland, collapsed as a train crossed, killing 75 people. Legend says that on every anniversary of the accident, a ghostly train is seen and the screams of its poor passengers are heard.

Ghost Stories

The pages of literature contain many stories of ghostly goings-on. Famous authors, including William Shakespeare, Charles Dickens and Washington Irving, have all written ghosts into their hugely popular stories.

Author Charles Dickens was so interested in ghosts that he joined the Ghost Club in the 1860s.

Victorian author, Charles Dickens, used ghosts as characters in several stories, including A Christmas Carol (see opposite), and The Signalman, the tale published in 1866 of a haunted railway worker who sees a ghost before each of three terrible accidents. From 1820 comes The Legend of Sleepy Hollow, written by American author Washington Irving. The story is set in a valley called Sleepy Hollow. Teacher Ichabod Crane is haunted by a headless horseman, apparently the ghost of a Revolutionary War soldier.

In this painting of The Legend of Sleepy Hollow from 1858, the Headless Horseman chases a terrified Ichabod Crane.

In William Shakespeare's Julius Caesar, Caesar is murdered by Brutus, who wants to control Rome. Later, Caesar's ghost appears to Brutus, saying that they will meet again on the battlefield. In Shakespeare's Macbeth, Macbeth kills King Duncan of Scotland. He also arranges for Banquo, a fellow general, to be killed. Banquo's ghost then alarmingly appears to Macbeth at a banquet.

The ghost of Caesar appears to Brutus in Shakespeare's play Julius Caesar.

Yotsuya Kaidan is a famous Japanese ghost story. In the story, the ghost of the Oiwa, a murdered woman, takes the form of a haunted lantern.

In Dickens' A Christmas Carol, four ghosts appear to Ebenezer Scrooge on Christmas Eve. They are Jacob Marley, his dead partner, and the Ghosts of Christmas Past, Christmas Present and Christmas Future.

Ghost Hunters

Think your house is haunted? If so, you need to call in a team of ghost hunters (or psychic investigators). They specialise in detecting ghosts, recording spooky sounds, taking photographs and videos, and measuring all sorts of ghostly phenomena.

A hand-held infra-red temperature sensor measures the temperature of remote surfaces.

Harry Price, ghost hunter of the 1920s

Ghost hunting began at the beginning of the 20th century, when the belief in ghosts and all things spiritual was popular. The most famous British ghost hunter of the time was Harry Price. Calling himself a paranormal researcher, he investigated the mediums, psychics and haunted houses of the time. In 1925, he set up the National Laboratory of Psychical Research. Price became a celebrity after his work at Borley Rectory (see page 15), where some of his team claimed to have witnessed ghostly goings-on.

Modern ghost hunters carry a whole range of equipment. Basic instruments include notebooks, torches, tape measures, sound recording equipment, video cameras and infra-red (night vision) cameras. They also carry thermometers, as ghosts are said to cool the air. A more advanced instrument is an electromagnetic field (EMF) meter, used by ghost hunters to detect the electromagnetic fields that ghosts are supposed to emit. EMF meters are sometimes used to trigger remote controlled cameras.

A ghost-hunting team investigates a haunted house. They are trying to find evidence of ghostly activity with their recording devices and instruments.

A medium summons a ghost.

Ghostly Celebrations

Dead souls terrify many people, but in some countries and cultures, ghosts are celebrated with special days and festivals, such as Halloween. The ghosts themselves are often invited to take part!

A sinister Irish Halloween Jack-o'-lantern, carved from a turnip

For thousands of years, the end of summer was celebrated in Britain on November 1. This date was also when people believed that the souls of the dead returned to Earth. They lit fires to ward off ghosts and wore disguises to stop ghosts of friends and relatives recognising them. This end-of-summer festival is known today as Halloween or All Hallows' Eve, when people dress up to celebrate all things spooky and ghostly. Halloween takes place on October 31 in Britain and the USA.

Traditionally, a woman can see the face of her future husband in a mirror on Halloween.

A Halloween celebration from the 1830s, with dancing and traditional games, such as bobbing for apples.